DALLAS
COWBOYS

KENNY ABDO

Fly!
An Imprint of Abdo Zoom
abdobooks.com

abdobooks.com

Published by Abdo Zoom, a division of ABDO, P.O. Box 398166, Minneapolis, Minnesota
55439. Copyright © 2022 by Abdo Consulting Group, Inc. International copyrights
reserved in all countries. No part of this book may be reproduced in any
form without written permission from the publisher. Fly!™ is a trademark and logo
of Abdo Zoom.

Printed in the United States of America, North Mankato, Minnesota.
052021
092021

Photo Credits: AP Images, iStock, Shutterstock PREMIER
Production Contributors: Kenny Abdo, Jennie Forsberg, Grace Hansen
Design Contributors: Candice Keimig, Neil Klinepier

Library of Congress Control Number: 2020919484

Publisher's Cataloging-in-Publication Data

Names: Abdo, Kenny, author.
Title: Dallas Cowboys / by Kenny Abdo
Description: Minneapolis, Minnesota : Abdo Zoom, 2022 | Series: NFL teams |
    Includes online resources and index.
Identifiers: ISBN 9781098224592 (lib. bdg.) | ISBN 9781098225537 (ebook) |
    ISBN 9781098226008 (Read-to-Me ebook)
Subjects: LCSH: Dallas Cowboys (Football team)--Juvenile literature. | National Football
    League--Juvenile literature. | Football teams--Juvenile literature. | American
    football--Juvenile literature. | Professional sports--Juvenile literature.
Classification: DDC 796.33264--dc23

TABLE OF CONTENTS

DALLAS COWBOYS

Rounding up **championships** and riding off with victories, the Dallas Cowboys are one of the NFL's best teams.

In their many years on the field, the Cowboys were the second team in NFL history to win five **Super Bowls**!

KICK OFF

The Dallas Cowboys were established in 1960. They missed the **draft** that season and would post losing records until 1965, when they finished 7-7.

The Cowboys became one of the
top NFL teams in 1966. They went
10-3-1 that season and won the
Eastern Conference title!

Dallas went on to lose the NFL title game to Green Bay, 34-27. But getting that close to the **Super Bowl** gave them the drive they needed to make it back.

TEAM RECAPS

The Cowboys made it to **Super Bowl** V after a successful 1970 season.

In a heartbreaking turn of events, the Baltimore Colts kicked a field goal in the final minute to win 16–13.

Things would end much better the following season. They beat the Miami Dolphins at **Super Bowl** VI, holding them to just 185 yards and no touchdowns!

With more than 100 million viewers at home and a packed stadium watching, the Cowboys won **Super Bowl** XII! They beat the Denver Broncos 27–10.

The Cowboys won three more **Super
Bowls** after the 1992, '93, and '95 seasons!
They seemed to win each game with ease,
with scores of 52-17, 30-13, and 27-17
respectively.

The early 2000s were not the team's strongest years. Midway through the 2006 season, Tony Romo took over at **QB**. The Cowboys went on to win six of their last 10 games for a 9-7 record.

The 2020 season started out rough. **Quarterback** Dak Prescott suffered a compound fracture to his ankle, ending his season. Cowboys fans know America's team will return to its **Super Bowl**-winning days.

HALL OF FAME

Quarterback Roger Staubach was named the **Super Bowl's** Most Valuable Player in 1972. He also helped the Cowboys come back to win in the fourth quarter 23 times! Staubach was **inducted** into the Pro Football Hall of Fame in 1985.

Emmitt Smith scored 986 points with the Cowboys, more than any other player on the team! He broke the NFL record for career rushing yards in 2002. Smith was **inducted** into the Pro Football Hall of Fame in 2010.

Troy Aikman played all 12 seasons of his career with the Cowboys. As **quarterback**, he helped the team win three **Super Bowls** while being named **MVP** of the XXVII Big Game! Aikman was **inducted** into the Pro Football Hall of Fame in 2006.

GLOSSARY

championship – a game held to find a first-place winner.

draft – a process in sports to assign athletes to a certain team.

induct – to admit someone as a member of an organization.

MVP – short for "most valuable player," an award given in sports to a player who has performed the best in a game or series.

quarterback (QB) – the player on the offensive team that directs teammates in their play.

Super Bowl – the NFL championship game, played once a year.

ONLINE RESOURCES

Booklinks
NONFICTION NETWORK
FREE! ONLINE NONFICTION RESOURCES

To learn more about the Dallas Cowboys, please visit abdobooklinks.com or scan this QR code. These links are routinely monitored and updated to provide the most current information available.

INDEX